MORRILL ELEMENTARY SCHOOL

34880000812656

DATE DUE

954.92   Cumming, David.
Cum
          Bangladesh
C.1

Alexnino

11-7-07

Bangladesh

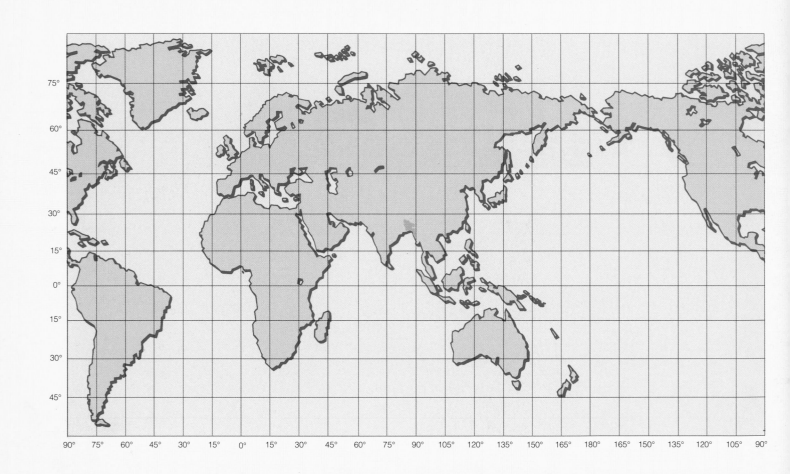

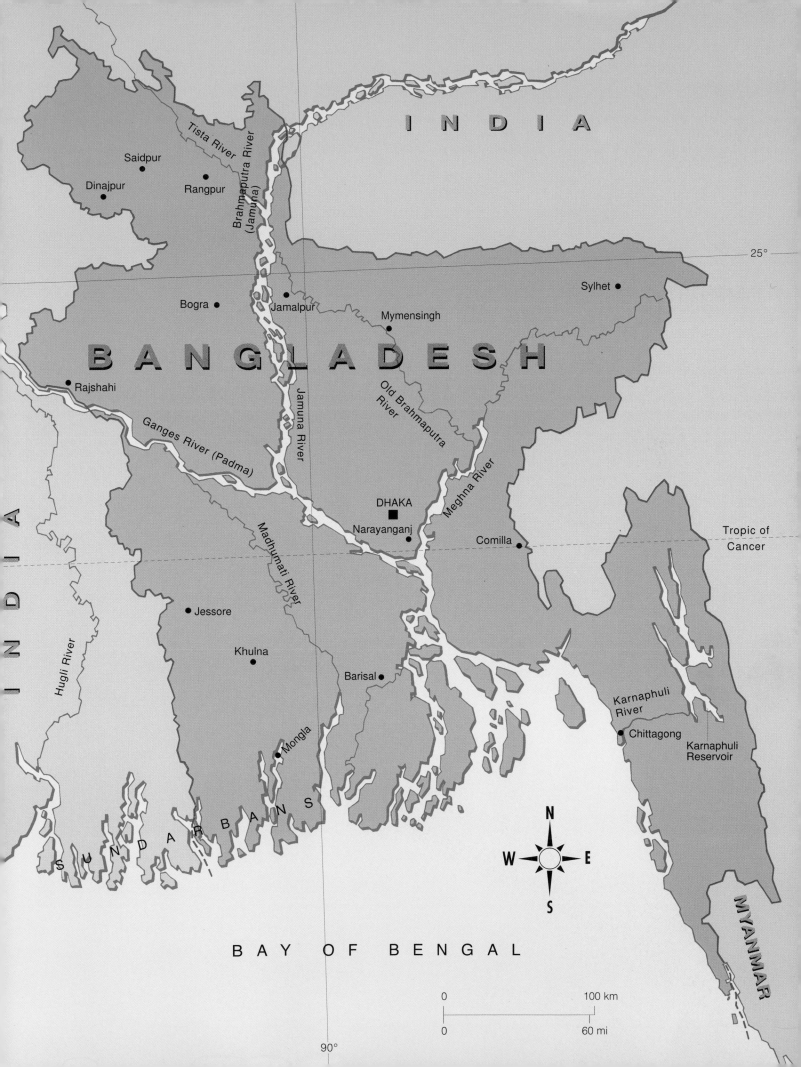

COUNTRY FACT FILES

Bangladesh

David Cumming

RSVP
RAINTREE
STECK-VAUGHN
PUBLISHERS
A Steck-Vaughn Company

Austin, Texas

© Copyright 1999, text, Steck-Vaughn Company

Published by Raintree Steck-Vaughn Publishers, an imprint of Steck-Vaughn Company

Design and typesetting Roger Kohn Designs
Commissioning editor Rosie Nixon
Editor Merle Thompson
Picture research Gina Brown
Maps János Márffy

We are grateful to the following for permission to reproduce photographs:
Front cover: Axiom, *above* (Jim Holmes); Panos, *below* (B. Klass); Axiom, pages 8/9 *above* (Jim Holmes), 14 (Jim Holmes), 24/25 *above* (Jim Holmes), 30 (Jim Holmes), 31 (Jim Holmes), 32 (Jim Holmes), 43 (Jim Holmes); Chapel Studios, pages 21 (Zul Mukhida), 29 (Zul Mukhida), 36 *below* (Zul Mukhida), 39 (Zul Mukhida), 40 (Zul Mukhida); David Cumming, pages 19, 33, 36 *above*; Ecoscene, page 18 *below left*; Eye Ubiquitous, page 16 *above left* (David Cumming); Life File Ltd, page 20 *below* (Stuart Norgrove); Christine Osborne, page 38; Panos, pages 8 *below* (Peter Barker), 11 (B. Klass), 12 (Trygve Bølstad), 13 *center left* (Jim Holmes), 13 *below left* (Z. Nelson), 15 *above left* (Trygve Bølstad), 15 *below left* (Jim Holmes), 16 *below left* (Mark McEvoy), 17 (Jim Holmes), 18 (Peter Backer), 20 *above*, 22 (Ron Giling), 23 (Ron Giling), 24 *above* (N. Cooper & J. Hammond), 26 *above left* (Peter Barker), 26 (Zed Nelson) *center right*, 27 (Ron Giling), 28 (Neil Cooper), 34 (B. Klass), 35 (Trygve Bølstad), 37 (Peter Barker), 42 (Jim Holmes); Science Photo Library, page 11 (CNES, 1990 Distribution Spot Image) above; Tony Stone, pages 10 (Ann Jousfrie), 41 (Tim Davis).

The statistics given in this book are the most up-to-date available at the time of going to press.

Printed in Hong Kong by Wing King Tong

Library of Congress Cataloging-in-Publication Data
Cumming, David.
Bangladesh / David Cumming.
p.   cm. — (Country fact files)
Includes bibliographical references and index.
ISBN 0-8172-5405-6
1. Bangladesh — History.   2. Bangladesh — Social life and customs.
I. Title.   II. Series.
DS394.5.C86   1999
954.92 — dc21   98-40725
CIP
AC

1 2 3 4 5 6 7 8 9 0 HK 02 01 00 99 98

C O N T E N T S

Words that are explained in the glossary are printed in
SMALL CAPITALS the first time they are mentioned in the text.

INTRODUCTION

Bangladesh was once part of the Indian state of Bengal. Hinduism flourished there for thousands of years before armies from Afghanistan brought Islam in the 1200s. In the 1500s, the Afghans were overthrown by another group of Muslim invaders, the Moguls, who had swept through northern India. In the 1700s, India was conquered by the British and became part of their worldwide empire. The British built roads and railroads in Bengal, but few factories or schools.

In 1947 India became independent. A new country of Pakistan was created from the two parts of India where Muslims were in the majority. So India became a homeland for Hindus, and Pakistan became a homeland for Muslims. The two parts of Pakistan were separated by nearly 1,860 miles (3,000 km) of northern India. Bengal itself was split, the western half remaining in India and the eastern half becoming East Pakistan. The British had built most of the

▼ *This government building is in the center of Dhaka, the capital city. It was built by the British and combines British and Indian styles of architecture.*

8

▲ *Like all Bangladeshi children, these girls often have to walk several miles to school or to shops, because there are few buses.*

BANGLADESH AT A GLANCE

- Area: 55,600 square miles (144,000 sq km)
- Population (1996): 123 million
- Population density: 2,220 people per square mile (854 people per sq km)
- Capital: Dhaka, population (1993) 6,105,500. It is estimated that, by 1995, it had risen to 7.8 million.
- Other main cities (1993): Chittagong 2,000,000; Khulna 877,000; Rajshahi 517,000
- Highest point: Mowdok Mual, 3,300 feet (1,003 m)
- Languages: Bangla (Bengali), English
- Major religions: Islam, Hinduism, Buddhism, Christianity
- Life expectancy at birth (1996): 56 years, compared with 76 years in the U.K. and U.S.
- Infant mortality (1996): 102 per 1,000 live births, compared with 6 per 1,000 in the U.K. and 8 in the United States
- Literacy (1995): men 49%, women 26%
- Currency: Taka = 100 paise
- Economy: highly dependent on agriculture, with a low level of industrialization
- Major resources: good farming land, timber, fish
- Major products: clothes, prawns, frogs' legs, jute, tea, leather, rice, newsprint
- Environmental problems: Sewage and industrial waste have damaged inland and coastal waters.

factories in the western half, so East Pakistan was left with little industry.

Although united by religion, West and East Pakistan soon became bitter enemies. For the East, rule by the British seemed to have been replaced by rule by West Pakistan. The final blow came in 1970, when the East's Sheikh Mujibur Rahman was not allowed to be prime minister after winning the elections. Talks to settle the issue broke down, and on March 26, 1971, Sheikh Mujibur Rahman announced that the East would become an independent country. After a brief period of conflict, Bangladesh came into existence on December 16, 1971. It was then totally separate from West Pakistan, which was renamed Pakistan.

Bangladesh started out with many political and economic disadvantages. A succession of natural disasters and bad governments has made its struggle to overcome them even more difficult. However, the people of Bangladesh are determined to pull through. They have been rewarded by improvements that would have challenged much richer nations, let alone one of the poorest.

◉ THE LANDSCAPE

◀ *Water is an important part of the landscape in Bangladesh. This photograph shows people washing in one of the many rivers that crisscrosses the country. The main rivers are marked on the map below. The Ganges and Brahmaputra are the biggest by far.*

Bangladesh occupies part of the northeastern corner of the Indian SUBCONTINENT. It is surrounded by India, except for a short border with Myanmar (Burma) and its 360-mile (580-km) coastline. Most of the coastline is not continuous, but broken up by the channels of a delta. The Ganges, Brahmaputra, and Meghna rivers flow through the delta and empty into the Bay of Bengal in the Indian Ocean. The Ganges and the Brahmaputra rivers start in the Himalaya Mountains. The Ganges starts in India, and the Brahmaputra begins in Tibet, China. In Bangladesh, the Ganges is renamed the Padma, and the Brahmaputra becomes the Jamuna. Together they drain 965,325 square miles (2,500,000 sq km) of land. Only the Amazon River and its tributaries carry more water to the ocean. But no other RIVER SYSTEM transports so much silt. The waters of the Ganges and Brahmaputra contain over two billion tons. Although the Meghna River contributes its share of silt

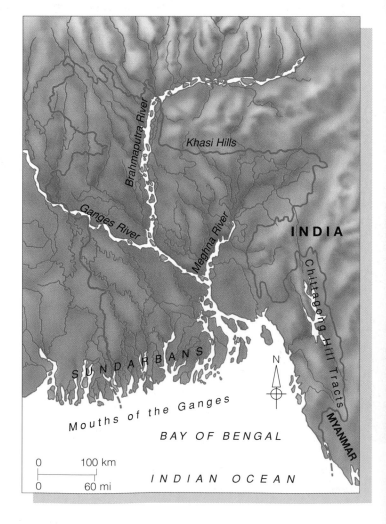

⑩

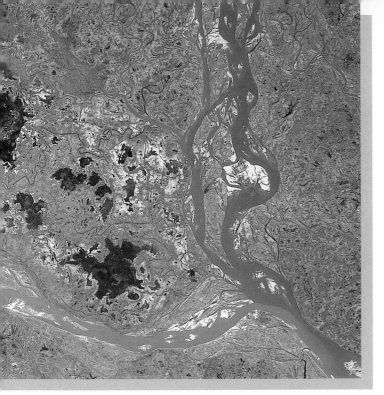

◀ *The Ganges (left) and Brahmaputra rivers viewed from space.*

was created. The highest points are the hills in the northeast and southeast.

Bangladesh is very open. Only about 15 percent of the land is covered with forests. These are on the Chittagong Hill Tracts in the southeast and in the Sundarbans in the southwest. Covering about 2,300 square miles (6,000 sq km), the Sundarbans stretches 50 miles (80 km) inland and over the border into India. Much of the Sundarbans is marshy land that is covered by water at high tide.

to the total load, it is insignificant when compared with that of the other two rivers.

All this silt is dropped as the rivers enter the Bay of Bengal. Over the centuries, it has built up to form the land on which the people of Bangladesh live. The land is very flat and low because of the way in which it

▲ *The Sundarbans, the world's largest river-mouth forest.*

KEY FACTS

● Bangladesh means "land of the Bangla-speaking people." *Bangla* is the local language, and *desh* means land.

● More than 75 percent of Bangladesh is less than 30 feet (10 m) above sea level.

● Bangladesh is the same size as the state of Illinois.

● The Ganges-Brahmaputra Delta is the largest delta in the world. It is more than twice the size of the Mississippi-Missouri Delta.

● The channel of the combined Padma, Jamuna, and Meghna rivers is 16 miles (25 km) wide at one point near the main mouth.

CLIMATE AND WEATHER

Heavy flooding turns Bangladesh into an inland sea, and life comes to a standstill. The damage can be enormous. People, animals, homes, and roads are washed away.

Bangladesh lies across the Tropic of Cancer, so it has a tropical climate. The year is divided into four seasons: autumn (October to November), winter (December to February), summer (March to May) and rainy (June to September). It is humid and hot all year-round. During the winter, temperatures drop to a pleasant 68°F (20°C), while in the summer they can reach an uncomfortable 95°F (35°C).

It is driest between October and May and wettest between June and September. Three times as much rain falls during this time than in all the other eight months combined. This rain is brought by winds, called the monsoon, which blow in from the Indian Ocean.

The monsoon usually starts in the middle of June. It is an unpredictable wind. Sometimes it comes early, sometimes late; some years it brings too much rain and other years too little. When there is a lot of rain, Bangladesh's rivers do not have the capacity to drain it all away, and they burst their banks to flood the adjoining land. These floods do little damage because

they are shallow and do not extend far. More serious flooding occurs when the monsoon's rain starts two or three weeks early. Then its arrival coincides with the water from the snow and ice melting in the Himalayas. The volume of water in the rivers is so great that the resulting floods are catastrophic.

The rainy season also brings fierce tropical storms, called cyclones, which form out in the Bay of Bengal. With winds of up to 125 mph (200 kph), cyclones wreak havoc on the coast, flattening everything in their way.

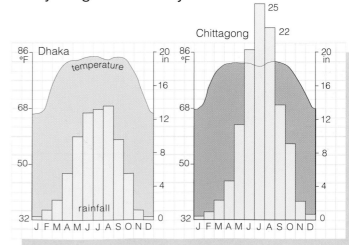

12

KEY FACTS

● The monsoon brings 80 percent of Bangladesh's annual rainfall.
● About 60 percent of Bangladesh's rice is grown during the monsoon season.
● On April 30, 1991, a severe cyclone killed between 140,000 and 200,000 people, when very strong winds and a 20-foot (7-m) high tidal wave hit the coast.

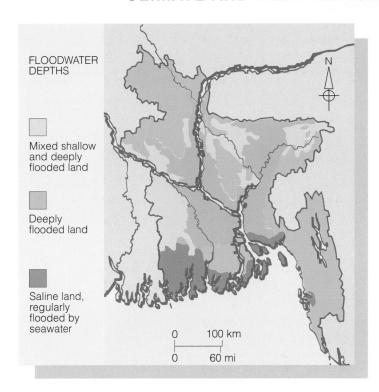

FLOODWATER DEPTHS

Mixed shallow and deeply flooded land

Deeply flooded land

Saline land, regularly flooded by seawater

0   100 km
0   60 mi

As the winds push the ocean into the shallows near the shore, towering tidal waves can rear up and crash down on the land, adding to the damage.

◄ *Strong shelters have been built on high ground. Whole villages can use them to escape floods and high winds.*

► *These men are strengthening a river embankment before the arrival of the monsoon rains.*

NATURAL RESOURCES

Bangladesh has few natural resources. In the northwest, near Rangpur, there are large deposits of limestone that are used to make cement, FERTILIZERS, and chemicals.

There are several small natural gas fields, the most recent of which were opened in 1994. Gas is piped from Sylhet to a nearby fertilizer factory, as well as to Dhaka and Chittagong. Small amounts of oil are also extracted near Sylhet. At Jamalgang, in the northwest, coal is mined, but not in large quantities.

As is true with most developing countries, Bangladesh is short of electricity. The southeast is powered by hydroelectricity from a dam across the Karnaphuli River. It provides about 10 percent of Bangladesh's total electricity. The rest is generated by power plants that burn either oil or gas. Since Bangladesh's own supplies are insufficient for this, foreign oil is required. Importing it is expensive, and as a result, there is little money left to build more power plants.

Bangladesh's forests have always been an important natural resource, because they have provided wood for building homes and for cooking. Their timber is also used for making paper. In 1995 Bangladesh produced 92,200 tons of paper. This was enough for its own needs and for selling abroad. Much of it came from a large mill in Khulna, which is supplied by the forests of the Sundarbans. High quality teak grows on the Chittagong Hill Tracts. It is made into furniture in local

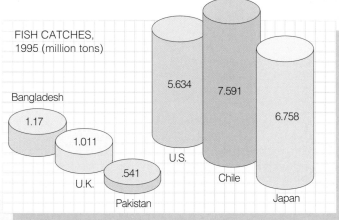

FISH CATCHES, 1995 (million tons)

Bangladesh 1.17
U.K. 1.011
Pakistan .541
U.S. 5.634
Chile 7.591
Japan 6.758

◄ *Bangladesh's many rivers provide its villagers with a plentiful supply of fish.*

► *Bamboo floats down the Karnaphuli River to Chittagong, to be made into furniture.*

14

▲ *The soil around Dhaka is good for making bricks. The sun is hot enough to dry them out, ready for use.*

KEY FACTS

● Building a dam across the Karnaphuli River created a 266-square mile (689-sq km) lake.
● In 1993 and 1994 prawns and frogs' legs together earned Bangladesh US$ 198 million. After jute and clothes, they were the third best exports.
● In 1995–1996, Bangladesh consumed 2,135,000 tons of oil.

factories, as well as exported.

Recently, the ocean has helped to create a thriving export industry—prawn farming. Prawns are bred in lagoons along the coast and in flooded fields. Farmers earn more from prawns than from rice, so they turn their fields into seawater ponds. Now frogs are also being farmed in ponds because their legs are in demand abroad as a delicacy.

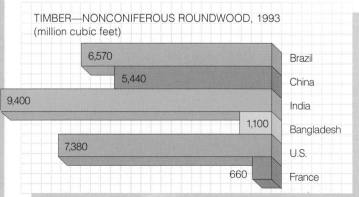

TIMBER—NONCONIFEROUS ROUNDWOOD, 1993
(million cubic feet)

Brazil	6,570
China	5,440
India	9,400
Bangladesh	1,100
U.S.	7,380
France	660

⑮

◖ POPULATION

Bangladesh is a very crowded place. The population has nearly tripled in the last fifty years. In the late 1940s, there were 754 people per square mile (290 per sq km); now there are over 2,210 (850).

There are several reasons for the increase. Bangladesh has a limited welfare system, so parents have needed children to look after them in old age. However, poor health care and a poor diet mean that many children die young. Parents in rural areas have a lot of children to ensure that some of them will reach adulthood. In a poor country like Bangladesh, parents also consider children to be valuable assets. Children can earn money, and the more

◀ *Today parents in the cities generally have only one or two children.*

▶ *These hill tribe people live deep in the forests, away from everyone else. Their survival is being threatened by logging companies who want to cut down the trees for timber.*

16

there are, the better-off a family will be. As a result there has been a high birthrate, and families have been large.

Since Bangladesh has few industries, most people have to work on the land. The amount of land has stayed the same, but the number of Bangladeshis who want to use it has increased greatly. The problem is made worse by inheritance laws and unfair distribution of land.

LAND SHORTAGES

When a farmer dies, his land has to be divided among his children (with sons, according to custom, receiving a larger

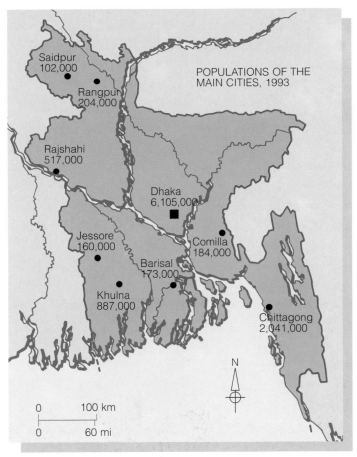

POPULATIONS OF THE MAIN CITIES, 1993

Saidpur 102,000
Rangpur 204,000
Rajshahi 517,000
Dhaka 6,105,000
Jessore 160,000
Comilla 184,000
Barisal 173,000
Khulna 887,000
Chittagong 2,041,000

N

| 0 | 100 km |
| 0 | 60 mi |

share than daughters). Consequently, as farmland is passed down through the generations, it is divided into smaller and smaller plots. Having a large number of children results in even smaller farms. Today 50 percent of farmers possess less than 0.5 acres (0.2 ha) of land (roughly the size of a tennis court). They can grow enough food to feed their families, but there is nothing left over to sell to provide an income. Their only option is to work for large landowners, which are few in number. Currently, 5 percent of the population owns 25 percent of the land.

◀ *The cities' slums are bursting with people, which means that families live in very crowded conditions.*

Many of these landowners have thousands of acres of land, which makes them rich and powerful. Most of them abuse their power, paying their workers little and hiring and firing them at will. Because they only need workers for a few months of the year to help with the planting and harvesting of crops, a small farmer cannot rely on them for a regular income, however little.

Even if a small farmer can obtain some extra land for growing crops to sell, the monsoon or a cyclone can destroy the harvest within minutes. The farmer is then forced to borrow from a moneylender at a very high rate of INTEREST. It is easy to run up a debt that will take years to repay. Many small farmers find it impossible to survive in the countryside.

OVERCROWDED CITIES

Every year, 5 percent of the rural population leaves the countryside. This means that nearly 5 million villagers arrive annually in Bangladesh's cities. These new arrivals want homes and jobs, both of which are already in short supply. Most end up working part-time, doing badly paid odd jobs for a few days a month. Home for them is a leaky shack in one of the shantytowns on the edge of a city. There, conditions are cramped and dirty, and disease is common.

Bangladesh's cities, especially Dhaka, have been changing as fast as they have been growing. Most of these developments,

▲ *The richest people live in Dhaka. Their houses are hidden behind walls and protected by strong gates.*

◀ *Dhaka is a city of great contrasts. This luxury hotel overlooks the shabby homes of some of the poorest inhabitants.*

18

▲ *A busy street market in the heart of Dhaka. Men usually go to the market to shop, because women are expected to stay home.*

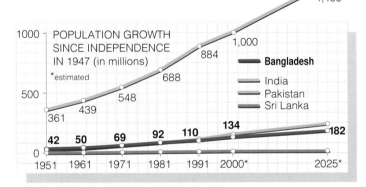

POPULATION GROWTH SINCE INDEPENDENCE IN 1947 (in millions)
*estimated

Bangladesh
India
Pakistan
Sri Lanka

KEY FACTS

● In 1993 there was 1 doctor for every 12,884 people in Bangladesh. In the U.K., there was 1 doctor for every 300 people, while in the United States there was 1 doctor for every 421 people.

● More than 13 million people live in shantytowns around the main cities.

● In Bangladesh, each woman has an average of 4 children. In the U.K., each woman has an average of 1.8 children, while in the United States the average is 2.1 children.

● The population of Bangladesh is increasing by 1.8% a year, compared with 0.3% in the U.K. and 0.9% in the U.S.

● There are 94 women for every 100 men in Bangladesh. In the U.K. and the U.S., there are 105 women for every 100 men.

● There are 10 million farms in Bangladesh, which have been divided into 59,850,000 plots of land.

however, have benefited the wealthy rather than the poor, who cannot afford satellite television or luxury hotels.

A NATION OF VILLAGES

Although millions have moved to the cities, Bangladesh remains a rural nation. It has 70,000 villages, where nearly 85 percent of the population live.

Village life has changed little over the years. It revolves around the farming calendar. Men work in the fields, looking after their crops and animals, while women stay at home, preparing meals and taking

care of the children and other household matters. Few homes have running water and electricity.

TRIBAL GROUPS

Bangladesh has twenty tribal groups, including the Chakma, Khasi, and Manipuri peoples. They make up less than 1 percent of the total population, and they farm on the hills of the northeast and southeast. They keep themselves separate so that they can preserve their centuries-old cultures and customs.

DAILY LIFE

RELIGION

Most Bangladeshis are Muslims, and Islam plays a prominent part in their daily lives. This is most obvious in the treatment of women. In Islam, males are given the dominant role in society. Husbands are expected to work to support their families. Wives are expected to stay at home; even going out alone is discouraged. This division of responsibilities means women are dependent on men, both financially and socially.

EDUCATION

The different treatment of men and women in Bangladesh begins when children are very young. Since girls are not meant to work, parents consider educating them properly a waste of time. Few girls are sent to secondary school, even though the government pays for most of the cost. As a result, 74 percent of adult women can neither read nor write. This places them

▲ *Strolling on the beach. This middle-class city family can afford a seaside vacation at the popular resort of Cox's Bazaar, south of Chittagong.*

▼ *These city children are fortunate to have some wasteland near their homes where they can play sports.*

PERCENTAGE OF PUPILS
ATTENDING PRIMARY
SCHOOLS, 1990 (ages 6–11)

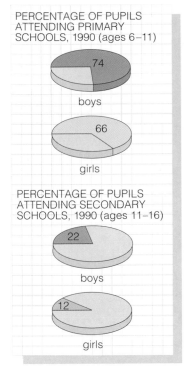

74
boys

66
girls

PERCENTAGE OF PUPILS
ATTENDING SECONDARY
SCHOOLS, 1990 (ages 11–16)

22
boys

12
girls

at a great disadvantage and gives men more power over them.

In Bangladesh as a whole, 62 percent of adults are illiterate. This is a reflection of the poverty there. Poor families cannot afford to let their children go to school instead of work. Although primary schools are free, only 70 percent of eligible pupils attend them. Of these children, only 25 percent will complete five years of basic education.

Overall, the most educated people in Bangladesh are generally men from rich families. Not only do these families appreciate the importance of a good education, they can afford to send their children to school.

EMPOWERING WOMEN

In Bangladesh, raising the status of women is being taken very seriously. It has been recognized that their social inferiority has been one of the stumbling blocks to

▲ *There are not enough schools, so classrooms are usually crammed with pupils.*

progress. "Empowering women" means giving them the means to influence and make decisions. In Bangladesh, this has involved teaching women how to read and write, giving them information on contraception, and encouraging them to form WORKERS' COOPERATIVES. Female empowerment has been effective. For example, because more parents are using birth control, and the size of families has

ADULT LITERACY, 1993 (%)

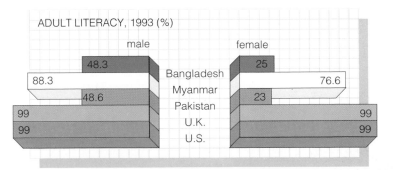

	male		female
Bangladesh	48.3		25
Myanmar	88.3		76.6
Pakistan	48.6		23
U.K.	99		99
U.S.	99		99

▲ *This young boy is helping his family by working. He is breaking stones for a new road.*

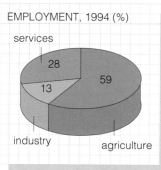

EMPLOYMENT, 1994 (%)

services 28
59
13
industry
agriculture

she wrote about the oppression of women in her book *Lajja* (*Shame*). She had to flee Bangladesh, but she has since returned home to continue the fight for equal rights for women.

HEALTH PROBLEMS

Classes in health and hygiene are also playing a part in the empowerment of women. Since the majority of women have received little education, they are unaware of even the simplest matters connected with taking care of their own and their children's health. Water can easily spread disease, so in a country where there are a lot of rivers, illnesses spread quickly. Sanitation is poor. There is a lack of sewage and water-treatment plants, toilets,

dropped, the population has been growing at a slower rate. With fewer mouths to feed, Bangladesh has more money available to modernize. Girls, too, are receiving a better education.

Inevitably, the empowerment of women has its critics. Most of these are men who think that it is damaging Islam. In 1993 Taslima Nasreen caused an uproar when

KEY FACTS

● In 1995 there were 84 newspapers in Bangladesh for every 1,000 homes. In the U.K., there were 108 newspapers for every 1,000 homes, and in the U.S., 104.

● In the same year, there were 83 televisions and 80 radios for every 1,000 homes in Bangladesh. In the U.K., there were 105 televisions and 110 radios for every 1,000 homes, while in the U.S. there were 111 televisions and 123 radios.

● In 1993 there were 2 telephones for every 1,000 people in Bangladesh. In the U.K., there were 494 telephones for every 1,000 people, and in the U.S., 574.

● One-half the houses are made of mud bricks and are without plumbing: one toilet may be shared by as many as 50 families.

● In 1994, 40% of married couples used birth control, compared with 19% in 1983.

● In Bangladesh, 5% of managers are women, while in the U.K. 33% are managers, and in the U.S., 42%.

● Education is free at government schools for all children ages 6 to 14.

and running water in homes. This means that the rivers are full of germs. Yet this is the water people have to use for washing. Telling women about the dirty water, together with giving them advice on how to keep food clean and to improve their diet, is helping to prevent illnesses. In the end, this will help people live longer. Even so, Bangladesh is still short of the doctors and hospitals it needs to improve things further.

LEISURE

The arrival of satellite television is beginning to undermine many long-held family values. Bangladeshi teenagers can now see how their contemporaries behave in other countries. This is making them question their own way of life. However, this is confined to the cities. In the countryside, few people can afford televisions. Their favorite pastime is watching a much bigger screen—in movie

▶ *In the cities, satellite television is giving people new ideas that are worrying the older generation.*

▲ *The Hindu festival of Bera is celebrated with boat races between local villages.*

theaters. The most common films are action-packed musicals with catchy songs that can be heard blaring out of radios. Soccer is the most popular sport, followed by volleyball and kabadi (a team game similar to tag). Children possess few things to play with, except for homemade kites and toys.

THE EXTENDED FAMILY

Considering all the obstacles to survival in Bangladesh, it is not surprising that the family as a group is important. By sticking together, it can survive tragedies that would defeat people on their own. In Bangladesh the family always comes before the individual, and many customs and practices ensure that this continues. For example, it is normal for several generations to live together under one roof as an extended family. Children are brought up to respect

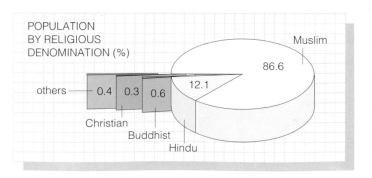

POPULATION BY RELIGIOUS DENOMINATION (%)

others — 0.4 | 0.3 | 0.6 | 12.1 | Muslim 86.6

Christian — Buddhist — Hindu

FESTIVALS AND HOLIDAYS

January 1	NEW YEAR'S DAY
(The date changes each year.)	RAMADAN (A period of fasting) Muslims mark the occasion when the Koran was revealed to the prophet Muhammad. The date of Ramadan varies each year, because it is based on the Muslim lunar calendar. Ramadan begins with the festival of JAMAT-UL-WIDA, and it ends with the ID-UL-FITR holiday.
February	SARASWATI PUJA A Hindu festival in honor of Saraswati, goddess of knowledge
February 21	NATIONAL MOURNING DAY In memory of those who died fighting in West Pakistan in the 1970s.
March	HOLI (The Festival of Colors) A Hindu festival celebrating the end of winter
March/April	GOOD FRIDAY AND EASTER MONDAY A Christian festival marking the death and resurrection of Jesus Christ.
March 26	INDEPENDENCE DAY A holiday in memory of the day on which Bangladesh declared itself separate from West Pakistan
April 14	PAHELA BAISAKH A Hindu festival celebrating the Bengali New Year
April 18	ID-UL-ADHA (The Feast of the Sacrifice) A Muslim festival when sheep and goats are slaughtered and given to the poor and when the traditional pilgrimage to Mecca (the Haj) begins
May 1	MAY DAY
May/June	BUDDHA PURINIMA A Buddhist festival when Buddha's birthday and his enlightenment are celebrated
May 9	MUHARRAM (The Muslim New Year)
July 18	ID-E-MILAD-UN-NABI A Muslim festival celebrating the birthday of the prophet Muhammad
August/ September	HINDU BERA A Hindu festival when models of the bera (a bird that is half falcon, half peacock) are put on small rafts, set on fire, and floated down rivers in honor of the god
September/ October	DUSSEHRA A Hindu festival celebrating Lord Rama's defeat of the demon-king, Ravanna DURGA PUJA A Hindu festival when images of the goddess Durga are put into rivers
October/ November	DIWALI The Festival of Lights, when Hindus mark Lord Rama's return from exile
November 7	NATIONAL REVOLUTION DAY A holiday celebrating the beginning of Bangladesh's separation from former West Pakistan
December 16	BIGANJ DIBASH (Victory Day) Marks the end of the independence war with West Pakistan
December 25	CHRISTMAS DAY
December 26	BOXING DAY holiday

◀ *The cool marble floor of this mosque makes it a pleasant place for a chat after worship.*

FESTIVALS AND HOLIDAYS

The two most important religious occasions are the Id-ul-Fitr and Id-ul-Adha festivals of Islam. The former marks the end of Ramadan (the month when Muslims fast). People dress in their best clothes to visit friends and family and give presents to children. Id-ul-Adha is the time when the annual pilgrimage to the holy city of Mecca, in Saudi Arabia, begins. Sheep and goats are killed, and the meat is given to the poor. The major festivals of the other religions are also celebrated by many people.

The main nonreligious holidays are Independence Day and Victory Day. Both are connected with Bangladesh's fight to separate from West Pakistan.

their elders, and to consult their parents and the head of the family before making any important decisions, including who they will marry. After his wedding, a son does not leave home. Instead he brings his bride back to join his family. A young married couple or single people living on their own is very rare.

25

RULES AND LAWS

Bangladesh is a parliamentary democracy, with a written constitution. Its single-chamber Parliament, the Jatiya Sangsad in Dhaka, has 330 members, 300 of whom are elected. The other 30 seats are reserved for women, who are appointed by the 300 elected members. The elections for Parliament are held every five years, and people have to be aged over 18 to vote.

The members of Parliament elect the president, who is the head of state. The president, too, is elected for a five-year term in office. He or she is responsible for appointing the chief justice and judges, including those who sit in the Supreme Court. The president is also in charge of the armed forces.

The president appoints the prime minister, the head of the government. The prime minister is usually the leader of the political party that has the largest number of seats in the Parliament. He or she governs Bangladesh with the help of a cabinet of ministers.

Bangladesh is divided into four divisions for local government purposes: Chittagong, Dhaka, Khulna, and Rajshahi. These divisions are subdivided into zillas

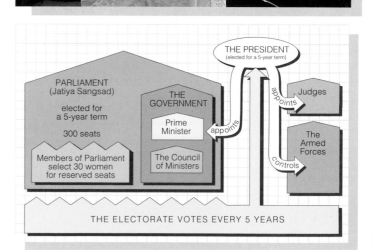

(districts), thanas (groups of unions), and unions (groups of villages), with elected councils at each level.

During its short life, Bangladesh has rarely functioned as a democracy and has

26

KEY FACTS

● In the national flag, the green background represents the greenery, vitality, and youthfulness of Bangladesh. The red circle symbolizes the rising sun of independence after the dark night of a bloody struggle.

● Bangladesh is a member of the United Nations, the Non-Aligned Movement, and the Organization of the Islamic Conference.

● The main political parties are the Awami League (socialist), the Bangladesh Nationalist Party (right of center) and the National Party (a coalition of five parties who want Islam to play a more important part in Bangladesh).

● At least 60% of Bangladeshis do not own any land. Governments have promised to break up large farms and redistribute their land, but rich landowners have always been able to stop them.

● It was only in 1996 that women were given the right to vote in elections.

HEADS OF GOVERNMENT

PRESIDENTS

1972	Sheikh Mujibur Rahman
1972–1973	Abu Saeed Chowdhury
1974–1975	Mohammadullah
1975	Sheikh Mujibur Rahman. In August Rahman was assassinated by the army and succeeded by Khondaker Mushtaq Ahmad. In November Ahmad was replaced by Brigadier Khalid Musharaf who, after 3 days, was overthrown.
1975–1977	Abu Saadat Mohammad Sayem
1979	Major-General Zia Ur-Rahman
1981	Zia Ur-Rahman was assassinated by the army and replaced by Abdus Sattar as president.
1982	Abdul Fazal Mohammad Ahsanuddin Chowdhury
1983–1989	General Hossain Mohammad Ershad. In 1989 he was forced to resign, sentenced to 20 years in jail, and charged with corruption.
1990	Shehabuddin Ahmed
1991	Abdur Rahman Biswas
1996	Shehabuddin Ahmed

PRIME MINISTERS

1972	Sheikh Mujibur Rahman
1975	Mohammad Monsur Ali
1975–1979	*MARTIAL LAW*
1979–1982	Mohammad Azizur Rahman
1982–1984	*MARTIAL LAW*
1984–1985	Ataur Rahman Khan
1986–1988	Mizanur Rahman Chowdhury
1988–1989	Moudud Ahmed
1989–1991	Kazi Zafar Ahmed
1991	Begum Khaleda Zia (the wife of General Zia Ur-Rahman)
1996	Zia was defeated in the elections, and Sheikh Hasina Wajed (daughter of Sheikh Mujibur Rahman) became prime minister.

often been in chaos. It has been run by a succession of all-powerful presidents and prime ministers supported by the army and officials who are often greedy. They have spent much of the time squabbling among themselves rather than governing. There have been many COUPS and countercoups. Two presidents have been assassinated and one imprisoned. Elections have been

canceled, political parties banned, and their leaders jailed. Furious, the people have paralyzed daily life with nationwide strikes and demonstrations.

In 1991 presidential rule was abolished, and Parliament and the prime minister had their powers restored in a return to democracy. However, Bangladesh still remains very unstable. The 1996 parliamentary elections had to be held twice because of complaints about fairness.

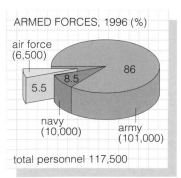

ARMED FORCES, 1996 (%)

air force (6,500) — 5.5
navy (10,000) — 8.5
army (101,000) — 86

total personnel 117,500

► *Demonstrations are a part of daily life in Bangladesh. These women want higher wages.*

FOOD AND FARMING

FLOODS AND THE SOIL

Bangladesh has a landscape with fertile soil suitable for farming. The silt deposited by rivers is rich in the nutrients that crops need in order to grow. Furthermore, the nutrients are topped up every year when the rivers flood and leave behind a new layer of silt in the fields. Thus, the flooding, which can cause so much damage, also does good, provided it is not too deep to wash away all the silt. Consequently, Bangladesh has some of the world's best farming land.

THE IMPORTANCE OF FARMING

Farming remains the most important activity in Bangladesh. It is responsible for 25 percent of all the wealth created there every year. About 65 percent of the total labor force works in farming, or in jobs closely connected with it. Nearly 25 percent of Bangladesh's EXPORT EARNINGS come from farming.

FOOD AND CASH CROPS

The two main crops, rice and jute, thrive in Bangladesh's hot, wet climate. Rice is the main food crop. In fact, Bangladesh is one of the world's largest producers of rice. About 80 percent of all farmland is used for growing it, and this land provides enough rice to feed the people. Wheat, potatoes, PULSES, and a wide selection of fruits and vegetables are also cultivated to eat.

Most of the rice is planted in June and July and harvested after the monsoon, in December and January. Farmers who are able to irrigate their fields by pumping water out of rivers or tube wells can cultivate a second crop during the dry season. They plant the rice in December

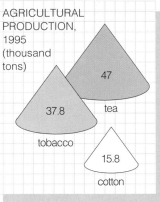

AGRICULTURAL PRODUCTION, 1995 (thousand tons)

- tobacco 37.8
- tea 47
- cotton 15.8

▲ *Young boys are catching fish that have been driven up to this wooden fence across a small river.*

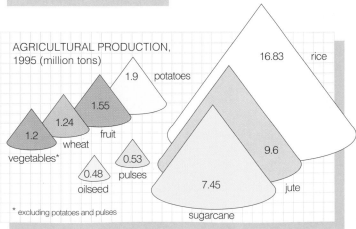

AGRICULTURAL PRODUCTION, 1995 (million tons)

- vegetables* 1.2
- wheat 1.24
- fruit 1.55
- potatoes 1.9
- oilseed 0.48
- pulses 0.53
- rice 16.83
- jute 9.6
- sugarcane 7.45

* excluding potatoes and pulses

28

and January and harvest it in May and June. The dry season is also the time when farmers grow other food crops, like wheat and pulses, which do not like wet conditions. These are planted in November and December and harvested in March.

Jute is the biggest cash crop. Its

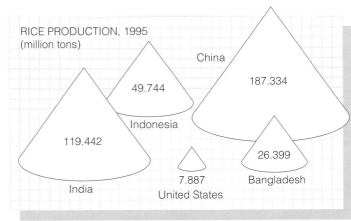

RICE PRODUCTION, 1995
(million tons)

China 187.334

Indonesia 49.744

India 119.442

United States 7.887

Bangladesh 26.399

cultivation was expanded during British rule because it was used to make sacks, ropes, and the backing material for carpets. Today 25 million people are involved in growing, processing, and selling jute. It is a major export-earner, second only to clothes. In recent years, however, it is becoming less important. Competition from human-made fibers is reducing the demand for jute worldwide. Since 1991, 22,000 jobs have been lost as a result of the government closing jute mills. The World Bank is giving the industry

▼ *These people are planting young rice plants in "nurseries." The plants will be transferred to paddy fields when they are bigger.*

US$ 250 million to modernize. This money is being used to buy machinery for making high-quality jute yarn, which is wanted by carpet makers in Turkey and Iran. Hopefully, this will prevent further mill closures.

Tea is the second most valuable cash crop. It is grown on hillside plantations around the northern town of Sylhet. Cotton, sugarcane, and tobacco are the other cash crops.

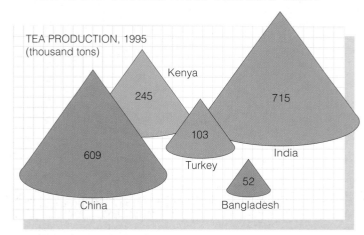

TEA PRODUCTION, 1995 (thousand tons)

China 609
Kenya 245
Turkey 103
India 715
Bangladesh 52

THE GREEN REVOLUTION

During the 1970s and 1980s, new high-yielding varieties of rice were introduced. The size of harvests was significantly increased. This was called the Green Revolution. It allowed farmers to increase rice production so that there was plenty to eat. Unfortunately, these rice varieties

▼ *Tea pickers on a hillside plantation near Sylhet. Most of the crop will be exported.*

30

KEY FACTS

● Eighty percent of Bangladesh is farmland.
● The new high-yielding varieties of rice have long stalks so that the grains can ripen above floodwater.
● Bangladesh is the world's fifth largest exporter of tea.
● On average, Bangladeshis consume 2,019 calories a day. This is only 87% of what they need to eat and drink in order to be healthy.
● Bangladeshis call jute "the golden fiber," because it earns them a lot of money from exports.
● There are 116 million chickens, almost 1 for every person in Bangladesh.

◀ *Bangladesh's climate and soil are good for growing a wide selection of vegetables, shown here in a local market.*

required large amounts of expensive chemical fertilizers and PESTICIDES to be successful. As a result, many poor rice farmers ended up in debt and had to sell their land.

FOOD AND DRINK

Since rice is plentiful, it is eaten every day. The most popular dishes are pulao and biryani. Pulao is boiled rice mixed with spiced vegetables, such as onions, peas, and carrots. Biryani is rice with meat or chicken. Because meat is expensive, only wealthy families eat it regularly. Fish, on the other hand, is common because people can catch it for free. Even if they have to

buy fish, there are so many in the rivers that it is cheap. Muslims are forbidden to eat pork and pork products, and to drink alcohol, so these are not available in Bangladesh. People have tea and soft drinks when they are thirsty.

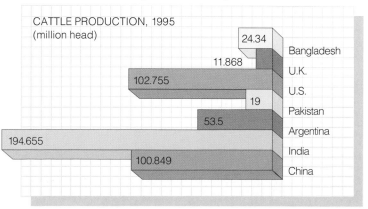

CATTLE PRODUCTION, 1995 (million head)

Country	Million head
Bangladesh	24.34
U.K.	11.868
U.S.	102.755
Pakistan	19
Argentina	53.5
India	194.655
China	100.849

● TRADE AND INDUSTRY

Industry provides only 10 percent of the wealth created every year in Bangladesh. It employs only 14 percent of all workers.

▲ *Jute has to be soaked in water before the fibers can be extracted.*

PAST AND PRESENT PROBLEMS

A combination of factors has held back the development of Bangladesh's industries. To start with, there are several physical hindrances. Bangladesh lacks the natural resources and energy that industries need. The climate and the landscape make communications difficult. The delta is criss-crossed by rivers that require expensive bridges if journeys are to be made shorter. Floods frequently make travel impossible.

History, both past and present, must also share some of the blame. The British did not want Bangladesh to industrialize and compete with British factories back home.

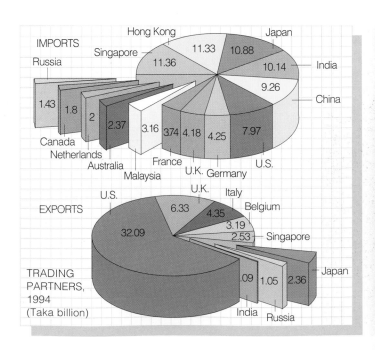

IMPORTS

TRADING PARTNERS, 1994 (Taka billion)

EXPORTS

32

They built mills to process jute, only because this made it easier to transport. West Pakistan behaved in a similar way after 1947, and blocked all its fellow countrymen's efforts at modernization. Since its own independence, Bangladesh has been poorly governed. As a result, the jute industry established by the British dominated the economy until recently. This was true both in terms of people employed and the amount earned from exports.

THE CLOTHING INDUSTRY

In the late 1970s, the government encouraged the textile industry to expand. By 1983 there were 47 factories, and by 1995 there were 2,100. Bangladesh had become the seventh largest clothes supplier to the United States and the main manufacturer of T-shirts and shirts for the European Union's member countries. Although it does not employ as many people as the jute industry, the clothing industry now earns about four times as much money from exports as jute. The only problem is that Bangladesh has to import much of what it needs to make clothes, from cotton to buttons and zippers, as well as the machinery. This added expense is canceled out by the savings made from low wages.

CHEAP LABOR

Its large population inevitably means that Bangladesh has a huge labor force. The supply of workers is so great that factory owners can get away with paying them very low wages. There is, however, always someone willing to accept the wages the employers are offering. Many of these workers are children from poor families, desperately in need of money. Children are employed because they are cheaper than adults, they complain less, and put up with working long hours in bad conditions. Working conditions are, however, improving, thanks to pressure from abroad. The government has recently introduced laws to ensure that working children are better treated.

◀ *This small shipbuilding yard near Dhaka builds passenger riverboats.*

► *This is one of
the many factories
in Dhaka where
clothes are made
for export.*

INDUSTRIAL CENTERS

Most industries are located in Chittagong,
which has the only oil refinery and steel
mill in Bangladesh. It also has factories
for freezing and tinning food; tanning
leather and turning it into goods such as
handbags and wallets; and for refining
sugar, and making cement, machine tools,
and cigarettes.

Dhaka is the most important industrial
city after Chittagong. It is the center of
the jute and clothing industries. Khulna,

the third largest industrial city, has jute
and paper mills, as well as cold storage
and fish-freezing factories. Sylhet also
produces paper and processes tea and
limestone.

TRADE AND AID

Most of Bangladesh's imports come in
through Chittagong, while the majority of
exports leave via the port of Mongla. The
main exports are clothes, jute and jute
products, frozen prawns and frogs' legs,
and leather and leather goods. The United
States, Western Europe, Singapore, and
Japan buy the bulk of these goods.

The main imports are factory machinery,
textiles, yarn to make clothing, petroleum,
and oil. Most of them come from
Singapore, Hong Kong, Japan, India,
and China.

Since Bangladesh has few industries,
it is difficult for it to earn enough money
from trade to survive without outside help.
Between 1971 and 1995, US$ 26 billion
has been pumped into Bangladesh to aid
its economy. Most of this money has been
loaned with the understanding that it will
be repaid with interest. This is usually

KEY FACTS

● The textile factories make 90 different
types of clothes.
● Skilled textile workers currently earn
$50 to $100 per month.
● In 1995 Bangladesh owed US$ 15.7 billion.
In the same year it earned US$ 2.7 billion
from exports. But it had to spend US$ 4.7
billion on imports, such as machinery, to
help make the things to export.
● In 1994–1995, US$ 1.2 billion was sent
back by Bangladeshis working abroad.

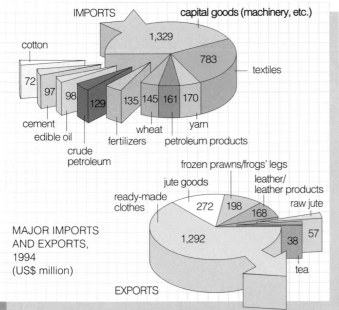

MAJOR IMPORTS AND EXPORTS, 1994 (US$ million)

IMPORTS

capital goods (machinery, etc.) — 1,329
textiles — 783
yarn — 170
petroleum products — 161
wheat — 145
fertilizers — 135
crude petroleum — 129
edible oil — 98
cement — 97
cotton — 72

EXPORTS

ready-made clothes — 1,292
jute goods — 272
frozen prawns/frogs' legs — 198
leather/leather products — 168
raw jute — 57
tea — 38

▼ *This is the largest and most costly fertilizer factory in Bangladesh. It opened in Chittagong in 1995 and cost US$ 510 million.*

calculated on a yearly basis. Thus, the longer it takes to repay a loan, the higher the final amount paid. Inevitably, all the obstacles hindering the country's progress have also delayed the repayment of loans. A point has now been reached where Bangladesh's future is being damaged by debt, and the money that was supposed to help Bangladesh is, in fact, harming it. The best way for this financial burden to be removed is to consider the money a gift. However, foreign governments and organizations are reluctant to write off these debts.

◼ TRANSPORTATION

The numerous rivers and the huge seasonal variation in their widths and depths has prevented the development of roads and railroads in Bangladesh. Because building bridges is too costly, ferries have to be used frequently. This means that journeys by road or rail take a long time, and monsoon floods can make them impossible.

RIVER TRAVEL

Most people and goods travel by water. Large and small passenger boats shuttle up and down and across the rivers, taking people to work and to visit families and friends. Small cargo ships distribute imported goods from Chittagong to Khulna and Dhaka, returning filled with export cargo to Mongla, where it is loaded on to oceangoing ships. The busy routes become so cluttered with craft of all shapes and sizes that it is easy to see why the rivers

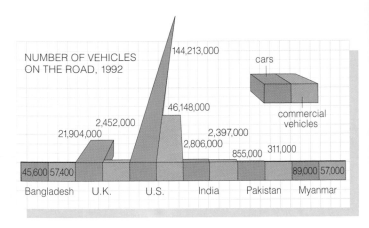

NUMBER OF VEHICLES ON THE ROAD, 1992

cars

commercial vehicles

144,213,000

46,148,000

2,452,000

21,904,000

2,397,000

2,806,000

855,000

311,000

45,600 57,400

89,000 57,000

Bangladesh   U.K.   U.S.   India   Pakistan   Myanmar

◀ **Small ferries take people across rivers.**

▶ **Rickshas fill the busy streets of Dhaka.**

◀ **These motorized rickshas and buses carry people to the outskirts of Chittagong.**

are referred to as the watery highways of Bangladesh. During the rainy months, 5,000 miles (8,000 km) of them can be used by medium to large-sized boats. An additional 11,200 miles (18,000 km) are open to small boats. In the dry season, the NAVIGABLE length of the rivers shrinks by half.

URBAN TRANSPORTATION

There are many bicycles and motorcycles in Bangladesh, but only the wealthiest people own cars. Most people rely on public transportation to get around. Pedal-powered rickshas are the most common and cheapest method of transportation around towns and cities. They can carry a family of four for very little cost. Rickshas can also be converted into freight carriers. They have become an indispensable part

of Dhaka's transportation system, carrying about 5 percent of the city's freight. They are also a mini-industry that provides work for thousands. In 1997 there were about 200,000 rickshas in Dhaka, more than in any other city in the world. One vehicle provides a job for two drivers, each one working a 9-hour shift. It is also estimated there are 100,000 people involved in repairing and manufacturing parts for rickshas. In addition to bringing all these advantages, rickshas help reduce Dhaka's vehicle pollution levels. Although they are a little more expensive than rickshas, buses are usually crammed, especially during the rush hours. Taxis are the most expensive form of urban transportation and are only used by the wealthy or by people in a hurry.

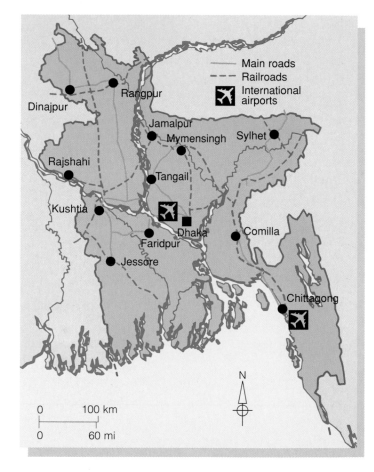

◀ *Very few Bangladeshis can afford to travel by their national airline.*

RAIL AND AIR

The railroads have been neglected for a long time, so the carriages are old and dilapidated, and the engines often break down. Bangladeshis prefer to travel across country by more reliable buses and

Map legend:
— Main roads
--- Railroads
✈ International airports

Cities: Dinajpur, Rangpur, Jamalpur, Mymensingh, Sylhet, Rajshahi, Tangail, Kushtia, Dhaka, Comilla, Faridpur, Jessore, Chittagong

Scale: 0 — 100 km, 0 — 60 mi

KEY FACTS

● In 1992 there were 8,470 miles (13,627 km) of roads, 5,310 miles (8,546 km) of which were paved.
● The most common means of motorized transportation in Bangladesh is the motorcycle. In 1995 there were 134,303.
● There are 5,240 miles (8,433 km) of inland waterways used for transportation.
● In 1992 there were 1,800 miles (2,892 km) of railroads and 502 railroad stations.
● Fifty-five million people and 2.5 million tons of freight are carried on the railroads each year in 20,142 carriages and wagons.
● Biman Bangladesh Airlines carried 667,000 passengers in 1993.
● The first ricksha arrived in Dhaka in 1938 from Calcutta, India.
● The first bridge across the Jamuna River has just been completed.
● The width of the Jamuna River varies from 1.6 miles (2.5 km) during dry months to 9.3 miles (15 km) during wet ones.

minibuses, even though there are long waits at ferry crossings, and the poor roads make travel uncomfortable.

The quickest, and also the most expensive, way around Bangladesh is on the aircraft of the small national airline Biman. It connects all the main cities with regular flights. Its planes also fly from Dhaka to many other countries.

THE ENVIRONMENT

THE WESTERN DELTA

In the early 1960s, India constructed the Farakka Dam across the Ganges River near its border with Bangladesh. The dam was designed to increase the amount of water flowing down the Hugli River, a tributary of the Ganges, which was collecting silt. While this helped to lower the amount of water entering Bangladesh during the monsoon, it also meant the Ganges was emptier during the dry season.

The western half of Bangladesh was the worst affected. As its rivers shrunk, the tide was able to push its way inland, filling the channels and underground reserves with seawater. The salt poisoned crops and drinking water. The west is also the driest part of Bangladesh, so its farmers rely on IRRIGATION. With little freshwater available for their fields, the soil turned to dust, which was easily blown away.

In 1985 a water-sharing agreement was made between India and Bangladesh to halt the damage being done by the Farakka Dam. The government of Bangladesh also began building a network of irrigation canals. These will distribute water from the Ganges around the western delta to bring it alive again.

POLLUTED WATER

Because raw sewage enters the rivers without being treated, the rivers contain a lot of germs. Industrial waste, often full of harmful chemicals, is also pumped directly

▼ *Women harvest potatoes in the dry soil of the western delta.*

39

into them. Since the Green Revolution, chemicals have drained off farmland treated with fertilizers and pesticides. Freshwater fish form an important part of Bangladeshis' diet. Not only is the polluted river water killing many fish, but it is also harming the health of people who eat the fish.

Pollution is at its worst along the coast near Chittagong. There oil tankers cleaning out their tanks have added to factory waste, creating a lethal combination of chemicals that has nearly killed ocean life.

Naturally the government is very concerned, but it does not have the money to build sufficient water-treatment plants to deal with the problem. Also, new anti-pollution laws are having little effect, because corrupt officials are turning a blind eye to those who are dumping waste.

KEY FACTS

● Bangladesh is home to 250 species of mammals, 200 kinds of fish, 150 varieties of reptiles and amphibians, and 750 types of birds.

● The Asian Development Bank plans to provide US$ 5 million in aid, in order to lower the pollution of the inland and coastal waters.

● Because the land in Bangladesh is so low, global warming would have catastrophic consequences if it were to cause a rise in the level of the world's oceans.

◀ *These plastic bottles will be recycled into new ones.*

▶ *The Bengal tiger was once nearly killed off by hunters. It lives in the Sundarbans, which is now a national park. It is a tidal region with many mudflats and mangrove swamps. Since it is not an easy place for people to travel around in, no one knows exactly how many tigers are living there. However, their numbers are increasing.*

WILDLIFE

Many species of animals and birds can be seen in Bangladesh, especially in the thick forests of the Sundarbans and the Chittagong Hill Tracts. The hills are home to elephants, leopards, deer, monkeys, parakeets, and mynah birds. But the animal Bangladesh is most proud of is the Bengal tiger, which lives in the Sundarbans. This has been turned into a national park where the Bengal tiger can live without being hunted to extinction.

41

THE FUTURE

Taking into account all its problems, Bangladesh has done remarkably well for a poor country. A rapidly expanding population used to put an enormous strain on its limited resources. It is now growing at 1.8 percent a year, down from a figure of 2.6 percent. This is a significant decrease for which women are largely responsible. Generally better informed and more confident about themselves, they have been instrumental in nearly halving the average size of families—from seven to four children.

With the aid of self-help organizations, such as the Grameen Bank and the Bangladesh Rural Advancement Committee (BRAC), women are spearheading a social revolution in the countryside. The Grameen Bank and the BRAC provide low-interest loans to women's groups. The money is channeled through women, because past behavior has shown that they are more reliable at repaying loans than men. The Grameen Bank, for example, has supported the building of 300,000 new homes. The BRAC helps to run 28,000 village schools.

Dealing with environmental problems has been more challenging. Cyclones cannot be stopped. However, with the

▼ *A social worker tells rural women about the benefits of pumped water over dirty river water.*

KEY FACTS

● In 1998 better health care and diet mean that people live 16 years longer and 54 fewer babies die out of every 1,000 born, compared to 1960.

● In 1998 the Grameen Bank began to provide every village with a mobile pay phone.

● Since 1993, with help from abroad, 650 cyclone shelters have been built.

▶ *These women run a savings program in their village. Here, they are receiving advice from a bank worker.*

help of satellites and radio broadcasts, coastal inhabitants now receive advance warning of their arrival, and they can take shelter. The Himalaya Mountains are outside Bangladesh, but their DEFORESTATION has caused SOIL EROSION. This has blocked up the delta's rivers and made them more prone to flooding. A multimillion-dollar flood-control plan, financed from abroad, has been under way since the early 1990s. Hundreds of miles of riverbanks will be strengthened and raised, but there is little agreement on whether this will reduce the flooding or make it worse.

Even if nature can be tamed, future progress depends on governments providing stability. This will attract foreign firms. With foreign investment, Bangladesh can provide more jobs and increase its exports to pay off crippling debts. It is the poorest who suffer the worst and who would benefit the most from a more prosperous Bangladesh. The Bangladeshis have an amazing capacity to bounce back from disaster and rebuild their lives. They are working hard for a higher standard of living in the future.

FURTHER INFORMATION

- AMNESTY INTERNATIONAL
304 Pennsylvania Avenue, SE
Washington, D.C. 20003

- EMBASSY OF THE PEOPLE'S
REPUBLIC OF BANGLADESH
2201 Wisconsin Avenue N.W., Suite 300
Washington, D.C. 20007

- OXFAM AMERICA
26 West Street
Boston, MA 02111-1206

- THE PERMANENT MISSION OF
BANGLADESH TO THE UNITED NATIONS
821 United Nations Plaza, 8th Floor
New York, NY 10017

BOOKS ABOUT BANGLADESH

Brace, Steve. *Bangladesh*. Austin, TX:
Thomson Learning, 1995.

Cumming, David. *The Ganges*. Raintree
Steck-Vaughn, 1993.

Lambert, David. *Asia*. Raintree Steck-
Vaughn, 1998.

Laure, Jason. *Bangladesh*. Children's
Press, 1992.

GLOSSARY

COUP
A violent or illegal change in government.

DEFORESTATION
The cutting down of large numbers of trees,
leaving the land bare.

EXPORT EARNINGS
Money earned from selling things abroad.

FERTILIZERS
Nutrients added to the soil that help plants
to grow. These are usually chemicals, but
there are also natural fertilizers, such as
animal dung.

INTEREST
Money that has to be paid in return for
receiving a loan. It is in the form of a
percentage of the amount originally
borrowed.

IRRIGATION
The process of bringing water to farmland
by means of pumps, canals, channels, or
ditches.

NAVIGABLE
A word used to describe a river that is deep
enough to be used by boats or ships.

PESTICIDES
Chemicals for killing insects that are harmful
to farmers' crops.

PULSES
Edible seeds, such as lentils, beans, and peas.

RIVER SYSTEM
A large river and all the smaller ones flowing
into it.

SOIL EROSION
The process by which topsoil is carried away
by the action of the wind or rain.

SUBCONTINENT
A large geographically or politically
independent part of a continent.

WORKERS' COOPERATIVE
A group of people who work together rather
than as individuals.

44

INDEX

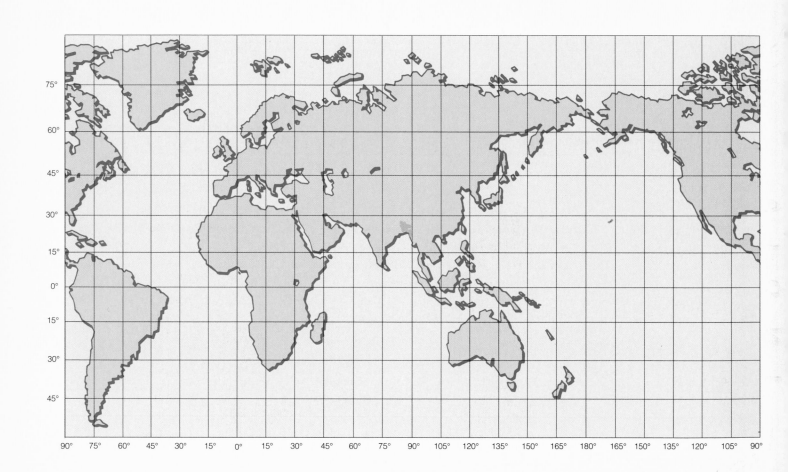